D1441141

APR - - 2015

THE LOCH NESS MONSTER

BY RAY McCLELLAN

EPIC

BELLWETHER MEDIA • MINNEAPOLIS, MN

EPIC BOOKS are no ordinary books. They burst with intense action, high-speed heroics, and shadows of the unknown. Are you ready for an Epic adventure?

This edition first published in 2014 by Bellwether Media, Inc.

No part of this publication may be reproduced in whole or in part without written permission of the publisher. For information regarding permission, write to Bellwether Media, Inc., Attention: Permissions Department, 5357 Penn Avenue South, Minneapolis, MN 55419.

Library of Congress Cataloging-in-Publication Data

McClellan, Ray.
   The Loch Ness Monster / by Ray McClellan.
      pages cm. – (Epic: Unexplained Mysteries)
   Summary: "Engaging images accompany information about the Loch Ness Monster. The combination of high-interest subject matter and light text is intended for students in grades 2 through 7"– Provided by publisher.
   Audience: Age 7-12.
   Includes bibliographical references and index.
   ISBN 978-1-62617-106-0 (hardcover : alk. paper)
   1. Loch Ness monster–Juvenile literature. I. Title.
   QL89.2.L6M33 2014
   001.944–dc23
                         2013037478

Text copyright © 2014 by Bellwether Media, Inc. EPIC and associated logos are trademarks and/or registered trademarks of Bellwether Media, Inc. SCHOLASTIC, CHILDREN'S PRESS, and associated logos are trademarks and/or registered trademarks of Scholastic Inc.

Designed by Jon Eppard.

Printed in the United States of America, North Mankato, MN.

TABLE OF CONTENTS

SPOTTING A MONSTER?

A **tourist** stands near **Loch** Ness in Scotland.
Suddenly, she sees a **blurry** shape in the water.
A large, dark form is moving under the surface.

03:23
2113.jpg
24M

113/113

The tourist grabs her camera. She takes a photo of the waves as the shape disappears. Did she just spot the Loch Ness Monster?

WHAT IS THE LOCH NESS MONSTER?

Loch Ness is one of Scotland's largest lakes. Its **murky** water has long been full of mystery. People report seeing a strange creature there.

THE DISCOVERY

The first sighting of the Loch Ness Monster was 1,400 years ago.

FAST FACTS ABOUT LOCH NESS

Width:

1 mile (1.6 kilometers)

Length:

23 miles (37 kilometers)

Depth:

almost 800 feet (244 meters)

N

W   E

S

● Loch Ness

SCOTLAND

Surgeon's Photograph
1934

A SIZE TOO SMALL
Scientists say that Loch Ness is too small for a creature this large.

Hugh Gray's photo 1933

Hugh Gray snapped the first photo of the creature in 1933. It showed a long tail. The next year, the "Surgeon's Photograph" was taken. This is a famous picture of the head.

Today, people call the monster Nessie. They think Nessie is a female. She is said to be 50 feet (15 meters) long!

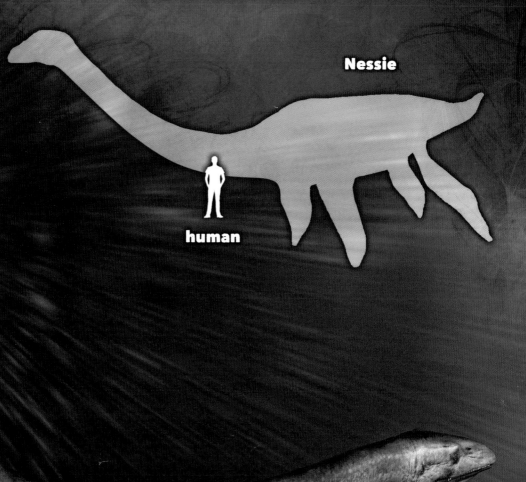

Nessie

human

SOMETHING IN THE WATER?

What could Nessie be? Many think she is a **plesiosaur** that survived in Loch Ness. Others think she is a seal, whale, or giant eel.

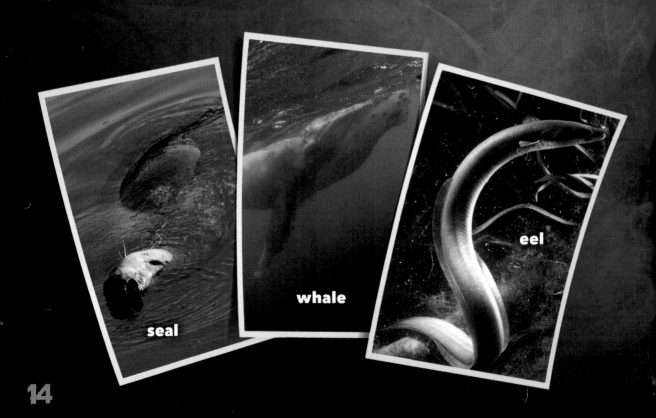

seal

whale

eel

plesiosaur

NOT EXTINCT?

The plesiosaur is
a reptile that lived
70 million years ago.

Skeptics think Nessie is an imaginary creature. They have proven that some photos of her are fakes.

Believers look for **evidence** of Nessie. They set up cameras to record videos of the loch. They also scan the waters with **sonar**.

IS THAT YOU, NESSIE?

A scan in 1987 tracked three objects deep in Loch Ness. Researchers were unable to determine what these large things were!

LOWRANCE

19

THE LOCH NESS MONSTER PROFILE

Names:
Loch Ness Monster, Nessie, Beastie, Kelpie, Water Horse

Home:
Loch Ness, Scotland

Length:
up to 50 feet (15 meters)

Weight:
up to 2,500 pounds (1,134 kilograms)

Colors:
black or gray

Features:
long neck, humped back

Swimming Speed:
up to 30 miles (48 kilometers) per hour

Nessie hunters will not stop searching. That much is certain. But is there really a monster deep in the water of Loch Ness?

GLOSSARY

blurry—not clear

evidence—physical proof of something

loch—lake; loch is the Scottish word for lake.

murky—dark and gloomy

plesiosaur—an ancient water reptile believed to be extinct

skeptics—people who doubt the truth of something

sonar—a system that uses sound waves to scan the water for objects and depth; researchers have used sonar on Loch Ness to look for Nessie.

tourist—a person who travels to visit another place

TO LEARN MORE

At the Library

Miller, Connie Colwell. *The Loch Ness Monster: The Unsolved Mystery*. Mankato, Minn.: Capstone Press, 2009.

Troupe, Thomas Kingsley. *The Legend of the Loch Ness Monster*. Mankato, Minn.: Picture Window Books, 2012.

Veitch, Catherine. *Sea Monsters*. Chicago, Ill.: Raintree, 2010.

On the Web

Learning more about the Loch Ness Monster is as easy as 1, 2, 3.

1. Go to www.factsurfer.com.

2. Enter "Loch Ness Monster" into the search box.

3. Click the "Surf" button and you will see a list of related Web sites.

With factsurfer.com, finding more information is just a click away.

INDEX

The images in this book are reproduced through the courtesy of: OSORIOartist, front cover, p. 8; bikeriderlondon/ Francois Loubser/ Alan Smillie, pp. 4-5 (composite); scyther5/ Yunaco, pp. 6-7 (composite); AridOcean, p. 9; AF Archive/ Alamy, p. 10; Mirrorpix/ Newscom, pp. 11, 17 (top); Victor Habbick, pp. 12-13, 15, 21; Paula Fisher, p. 14 (left); Joost van Uffelen, p. 14 (middle); Biosphoto/ SuperStock, p. 14 (right); Ballista/ Wikipedia, pp. 16-17; F1 Online/ SuperStock, p. 17 (bottom); Tom Stoddart/ Getty Images, pp. 18-19.